TABLE OF CONTENTS

Novel-Ties® are printed on recycled paper.

Copyright © 1989, 2003, 2010, 2012 by LEARNING LINKS

For the Teacher

This reproducible study guide to use in conjunction with the book *Mr. Popper's Penguins* consists of lessons for guided reading. Written in chapter-by-chapter format, the guide contains a synopsis, pre-reading activities, vocabulary and comprehension exercises, as well as extension activities to be used as follow-up to the novel.

In a homogeneous classroom, whole class instruction with one title is appropriate. In a heterogeneous classroom, reading groups should be formed: each group works on a different novel at its reading level. Depending upon the length of time devoted to reading in the classroom, each novel, with its guide and accompanying lessons, may be completed in three to six weeks.

Begin using NOVEL-TIES for reading development by distributing the novel and a folder to each child. Distribute duplicated pages of the study guide for students to place in their folders. After examining the cover and glancing through the book, students can participate in several pre-reading activities. Vocabulary questions should be considered prior to reading a chapter; all other work should be done after the chapter has been read. Comprehension questions can be answered orally or in writing. The classroom teacher should determine the amount of work to be assigned, always keeping in mind that readers must be nurtured and that the ultimate goal is encouraging students' love of reading.

The benefits of using NOVEL-TIES are numerous. Students read good literature in the original, rather than in abridged or edited form. The good reading habits, formed by practice in focusing on interpretive comprehension and literary techniques, will be transferred to the books students read independently. Passive readers become active, avid readers.

SYNOPSIS

Mr. Popper, an ordinary housepainter, who lives with his wife and children in suburban Stillwater, dreams of adventures at the North and South Poles. As a student of these regions, he has written to Admiral Drake, leader of an Antarctic exploring party. To Mr. Popper's delight, Admiral Drake acknowledges the letter at the beginning of a radio broadcast from the South Pole and surprises Mr. Popper with a penguin sent directly from Antarctica.

The inquisitive penguin, named Captain Cook, after the famous early Antarctic explorer, soon becomes an endearing member of the family. After some clever refrigerator reconstruction, the penguin is able to live comfortably in the Popper home. A policeman warns the Poppers that the penguin requires a city license, but Mr. Popper gives up his attempt to adhere to the law when no one at city hall comprehends his problem.

Captain Cook builds a nest for himself in the refrigerator by collecting sundry household items. When Mr. Popper takes Captain Cook for a walk, the penguin pecks at Mrs. Callahan's striped stockings and has his picture taken by some newspapermen, drawing a large crowd wherever he goes. After the penguin creates bedlam in the barbershop, Mr. Popper takes him home in a taxi.

Just as newspaper stories make a celebrity of the penguin, he becomes ill. Mr. Popper writes to the curator of a great aquarium for advice. In response, the curator ships him Greta, another penguin who seems to be suffering from similar symptoms of loneliness. When cold weather comes, the Poppers keep ice and snow in their house so that the penguins will be happy.

After Mr. Popper has an expensive freezing plant installed in the basement, Greta lays ten eggs. When the penguins hatch, Mr. Popper adds a swimming pool stocked with fish for the penguins to eat. To solve the family's growing financial problems, Mr. Popper decides to train the penguins to appear in the theater. When he has taught the penguins various tricks, he takes them by bus to see Mr. Greenbaum, owner of the Palace Theater. "Popper's Performing Penguins" get their big break when they go to the theater to audition: Mr. Greenbaum allows them to be a last-minute replacement act.

The penguins are a hit. The Poppers take them on the road and money begins to pour in: the penguins become more and more famous, but they are not popular with the other entertainers whose acts they disrupt.

One warm April day, Mr. Popper accidentally takes the penguins to the wrong theater, where they wreak havoc and are arrested. The penguins become weaker each day in the hot prison. Then to Mr. Popper's astonishment, Admiral Drake, newly returned from his expedition, arrives to obtain their release. He suggests that Mr. Popper allow him to start a race of penguins at the North Pole. Mr. Popper reaches an agonizing decision: he refuses a lucrative film offer and decides to give the penguins to Admiral Drake to take to the North Pole. Mr. Popper will return to his former occupation as house painter.

As Mr. Popper is bidding a tearful farewell to the penguins, Admiral Drake invites him to go along on the trip. An understanding Mrs. Popper gives Mr. Popper her cheerful permission.

BACKGROUND INFORMATION

Penguins

Penguins are birds that are incapable of flight. Although they are most at home in the water, they lay eggs and raise their young on land. Species of penguins live in Antarctica, South Africa, Australia, and parts of South America. Two species of penguins that live in the Antarctic are the Adélie penguin and the Emporer penguin. The Adélie penguin is small, weighing nine to fourteen pounds, while the Emporer penguin is much larger, weighing from fifty to two-hundred pounds.

The Arctic

The Arctic is the region of continuous cold around the North Pole. It includes the Arctic Ocean, thousands of islands, and the northern parts of the continents of Europe, Asia, and North America. The sun never shines on much of the Arctic during the winter. However, it shines on the entire region for part of the day from March to September.

Antarctica

Antarctica is the continent surrounding the South Pole. Most of Antarctica's land lies beneath one mile of snow. The interior is desolate and lifeless, but the seacoast abounds with animal life. There are seals, whales, penguins, petrels, and many other birds and fish.

Sir Francis Drake

Sir Francis Drake was an English admiral who lived from 1541 to 1596. He was commander of the Pelican, a ship later named the Golden Hind. His many travels including a slaving voyage from Guinea to South America interrupted by battle with Spaniards and voyages designed for exploration of the South American coast. He may have come ashore as far north as a bay near what is now San Franscisco, California, but the authenticity of a plaque supposedly left in "Drake's Bay" north of San Francisco, is questionable. Queen Elizabeth I requested that Drake look for a western exit to the Northwest Passage. During his search, he discovered a strait, now named after him, which proved that Tierra del Fuego was an island.

James Cook

James Cook, the first of the truly scientific navigator-explorers, lived from 1728 to 1779. He is known for his exploration of both the Pacific and Atlantic Oceans and his charting of the North American coast during three great voyages. He contributed extensively to the body of knowledge about the southern hemisphere.

PRE-READING ACTIVITIES

1. Preview the book by reading the title and the author's name and by looking at the illustration on the cover. Look at the illustrations inside the book. What do you think the book will be about? Do you expect it to be funny or serious, realistic or fantastic?

2. **Science Connection:** Read the Background Information on penguins on page two of this study guide and do some additional research to learn more about these interesting birds. As you read *Mr. Popper's Penguins*, determine how much you read about penguins is factual and how much is fantasy.

3. Notice the copyright date of this book which can be found opposite the Table of Contents. What qualities do you think a book must have to be in print for so many years?

4. **Social Studies Connection:** Locate the following areas on a globe or world atlas: the Arctic, Antarctica, India, the Himalayas, and the South Seas. What do you know about each area? What does the geography of each region suggest about its living conditions?

5. Read the Background Information on Sir Francis Drake and James Cook on page two of this study guide. Do some additional research on the lives of these two men as well as the following people to find out how they influenced the history of world exploration:

   - Christopher Columbus
   - Ferdinand Magellan
   - Lord Nelson
   - Queen Victoria

6. Create a pet owner's chart, such as the one below. After an informal survey of your classmates, fill in the information required.

Student's Name	Kind of Pet	Care Required

After the chart has been completed, determine which is the most popular kind of pet, which pets need the most care, and what is the most unusual household pet owned by a classmate.

CHAPTER 1, 2

Vocabulary: Draw a line from each word on the left to its definition on the right. Then use the numbered words to fill in the blanks in the sentences below.

1. bungalow
2. expedition
3. authority
4. prospect
5. missionary
6. expanse
7. spectacles

a. trip made for a specific purpose, such as exploration
b. eyeglasses
c. expectation; a looking forward
d. expert on a subject
e. large open area
f. cottage; small house
g. person sent by a church into an area to bring about religious and social change

. . . .

1. The family bought hiking boots and lightweight knapsacks to prepare for a mountain-climbing _____.

2. Use your _____ to read the small print on the map.

3. From his perch atop the mast, all the sailor could see was a great _____ of sea.

4. If you want to know why ants live and work in colonies, talk to Dr. Busybee, a(n) _____ on insects.

5. Instead of going camping this summer, we could rent a little _____ by the shore.

6. The children were pleased at the _____ of an entire weekend of fun without chores.

7. The young _____ was challenged by the idea of bringing the opportunity to worship to people who had left the forest.

> Read to find out why Mr. Popper prefers penguins to painting.

Questions:

1. What does Mr. Popper regret in his life?
2. What does Mr. Popper do to satisfy his interest in distant places?
3. Why does Mrs. Popper worry about her family during the winter months?
4. What surprising information does Mr. Popper learn about penguins? What theory does he develop about them?
5. Why is Mrs. Popper astonished when she listens to the radio with her husband on the night of September 29th?

Chapter 1, 2 (cont.)

Questions for Discussion:

1. Do you think Mr. Popper is an unhappy man? Would you like to have him as a friend or neighbor?

2. What do you learn about Mr. and Mrs. Popper's life that shows that they live in the 1930s and not in the present?

Literary Element: Characterization

Choose a word from the Word Box that best describes Mr. Popper in each of the following statements. Write the word you choose on the line below the statement.

WORD BOX			
absent-minded	amiable	impractical	inquisitive

1. Mr. Popper thought it would have been nice if he could have traveled around the world before he settled down.

   _____

2. Once Mr. Popper painted three kitchen walls green, and the fourth wall yellow.

   _____

3. While Mrs. Popper worried about the long winter ahead, Mr. Popper thought about how nice it would be to have a whole winter to read travel books without being interrupted by work.

   _____

4. When describing the Drake Expedition to Mrs. Popper, he said, "But I think the nicest part of all is the penguins. No wonder all the men on that expedition had such a good time playing with them."

   _____

Writing Activity:

Imagine you are Mr. Popper and use your research on penguins as the basis for a letter to Admiral Drake in which you express your theory about penguins.

CHAPTERS 3, 4

Vocabulary: Draw a line from each word on the left to its meaning on the right. Then answer the questions about the underlined words below.

1. waistcoat
2. meek
3. debris
4. trill
5. tobogganed
6. glare

a. rubble; trash
b. stare with a fierce or angry look
c. yielding; unassuming
d. coasted on a long, narrow sled made of thin board curved upward at the front
e. sing or play with a quavering effect
f. vest

. . . .

1. Why do people say that a penguin looks like it is wearing a waistcoat and a tuxedo jacket?

_____

_____

2. What is something you might ask for meekly?

_____

_____

3. What might you do with household debris?

_____

_____

4. If something trilled near you house, what might it be?

_____

_____

5. If someone tobogganed by your window, what season would it probably be?

_____

_____

6. What might cause your teacher to glare at you?

_____

_____

Read to find out how Mr. Popper gets a penguin of his own.

Chapters 3, 4 (cont.)

Questions:

1. How does a penguin come to live in Mr. Popper's home?
2. Why does Mr. Popper name the penguin Captain Cook?
3. Compare the way the children react to the penguin with the way Mrs. Popper reacts. Why does Mrs. Popper's attitude change?
4. What trouble does Captain Cook get into? Why does this happen?
5. What will Mr. Popper do to make the penguin comfortable?

Question for Discussion:

How do you think you and members of your family would react if a penguin were delivered to your home?

Science Connection:

Based upon your research on penguins, the Background Information on page two of this study guide, and the chapters you read in *Mr. Popper's Penguins*, what species of penguin did Mr. Popper receive from Admiral Drake? What facts do you know about this species that Mr. Popper may not know yet?

Activity: Reality – Fantasy

This story is a wonderful blend of the real and the make-believe. On the chart below, list those things in the story so far that are real and those things that are imaginary. Add to the chart as you read the book.

Reality	Fantasy

Writing Activity:

Write about something that actually happened to you, but add one amusing element of fantasy to the actual event.

CHAPTERS 5, 6

Vocabulary: Draw a line from each word on the left to its meaning on the right. Then use the numbered words to fill in the blanks in the sentences below.

1.	marketing	a.	made over or renovated
2.	indignant	b.	public order or regulation
3.	remodeled	c.	shopping
4.	municipal	d.	feeling displeasure about something unjust
5.	ordinance	e.	having to do with the local government of a town or city
6.	ventilating	f.	admitting a flow of fresh air

. . . .

1. José became _____ because he had more chores to do than his sister.

2. The Browns _____ their house to suit the needs of their growing family.

3. A town _____ required that wild animals be kept in cages.

4. You cannot vote in _____ elections if you live outside the village boundaries.

5. I prefer to go _____ at a supermarket, rather than at small stores.

6. Fans were installed to solve the problem of _____ the attic.

> Read to find out whether Mr. Popper needs a penguin license.

Questions:

1. Why does the refrigerator service man think Mr. Popper is crazy?

2. What causes the "shower of flying tools" and the "violent slamming of the door" by the refrigerator service man?

3. Why does a policeman come to the Poppers' house? What is the result of his visit?

4. Why does Mr. Popper give up trying to get a license for his penguin?

Chapters 5, 6 (cont.)

Questions for Discussion:

1. What kinds of animals might require licenses? For what other kinds of animals, in addition to penguins, might Mr. Popper *not* obtain a license?

2. Do you think people should try to domesticate wild animals or make pets of unusual species?

Activity: Readers Theatre

It is fun to read a story with dialogue as though it were a play. Read Chapters Five and Six aloud with your classmates taking the following parts:

- Refrigerator service man
- Mr. Popper
- Penguin
- Bill
- Janie
- Policeman
- Voices on the telephone

One student can read the narration; the characters should read only those words inside the quotation marks. Ignore phrases such as "he said" or "she said." You may want to use some simple props, such as hats and a telephone.

Writing Activity:

Imagine that you are Mr. Popper and you decide to make an appointment with a veterinarian to get the proper shots for your pet. Write the dialogue for the phone conversation that you have with the veterinarian's secretary, who will certainly be astonished by your request.

CHAPTERS 7, 8

Vocabulary: Synonyms are words with similar meanings. Draw a line from each word in column A to its synonym in column B. Then use the words in column A to fill in the blanks in the sentences below.

<u>A</u>

<u>B</u>

1. reluctantly
2. belated
3. idle
4. abandoned
5. reproach
6. extinct
7. bystander

a. overdue
b. lazy
c. scold
d. vanished
e. hesitantly
f. spectator
g. deserted

. . . .

1. You cannot _____ me for ignoring a rule I was never taught.

2. As a(n) _____ at the scene of the accident, I told the police what I saw.

3. Knowing the pool was very cold, I dove in _____.

4. Although I appear to be _____, I am really spending my time thinking about important issues.

5. Adults today worry that future generations will never see animals that are allowed to become _____.

6. After being _____ by its mother, the little kitten seemed pleased to be adopted by a family with children.

7. A(n) _____ birthday wish is better than none at all.

> Read to find out how the penguin changes life for the Poppers.

Questions:

1. How does Mr. Popper explain the penguin's collection of odd items?
2. Why does Mr. Popper think the penguin will be a big help to Mrs. Popper around the house?
3. Why does Mr. Popper suddenly dress and groom himself more carefully?
4. What are some of the animals for whom the penguin is mistaken as he walks with Mr. Popper?
5. Why does Mr. Popper find it difficult to take the penguin for a walk?

Chapters 7, 8 (cont.)

Question for Discussion:

If the penguin were to collect items for its rookery in your classroom or in a room of your home, what would it find?

Literary Devices:

I. *Foreshadowing*—When an author provides the reader with a clue to what will happen later on in the story, it is called foreshadowing. What do you think the last line in Chapter Eight foreshadows?

> The man who had kept the barbershop had, up to this time, been a very good friend of Mr. Popper's.

_____

_____

II. *Simile*—A simile is a figure of speech in which two unlike objects are compared using the words "like" or "as." For example:

> Never again would Mrs. Popper have to reproach him for looking as wild as a lion.

What is being compared?

_____

What does this suggest about Mr. Popper's former appearance?

_____

_____

Writing Activity:

Write a news article that the two reporters might have written after they saw Mr. Popper with the penguin and interviewed him on the street.

CHAPTERS 9, 10

Vocabulary: Analogies are equations in which the first pair of words has the same relationship as the second pair of words. For example: BLACK is to WHITE as HOT is to COLD. Both pairs of words are opposites. Circle the letter of the word you choose to complete the following analogies.

1. EXHAUSTION is to WEARINESS as DAZE is to _____.

    a. breakfast   b. spectacle   c. stupor   d. fatigue

2. ORANGE is to JUICE as SOAP is to _____.

    a. lather   b. clean   c. water   d. scented

3. NAUGHTY is to MISCHIEVOUS as _____ is to EXUBERANT.

    a. solemn   b. boisterous   c. sympathetic   d. fortunate

4. MANAGER is to STORE as _____ is to AQUARIUM.

    a. shark   b. visitor   c. tank   d. curator

5. _____ is to BED as SITTING is to SOFA.

    a. quilt   b. pillows   c. reclining   d. dreaming

Read to find out why the Poppers think about getting a second penguin.

Questions:

1. Why is the penguin an unwelcome visitor to the barber shop?
2. Why does Mr. Popper have to take a nap after his walk with the penguin?
3. Why is Chapter Ten titled, "Shadows"?
4. Why does Greta come to live with the Poppers?

Questions for Discussion:

1. What kind of store might be safe for the penguin to visit?
2. Do you think that a second penguin will have a good effect on the first penguin?

Writing Activity:

Write a short episode to describe what you think will happen when Greta arrives. Then compare your version with what actually happens in the book.

CHAPTERS 11, 12

Vocabulary: Draw a line from each word on the left to its definition on the right. Then use the numbered words to fill in the blanks in the paragraph below.

1. sleek
2. droll
3. astonished
4. occupied
5. blizzard
6. rookery

a. storm with driving snow, strong winds, and intense cold
b. busy
c. breeding place or colony of birds, such as penguins
d. smooth or glossy
e. surprised; startled
f. amusing in an odd way; witty

. . . .

On a summer day in Stillwater, everyone was _____ [1] in their usual pastimes. They were _____ [2] to see Mr. Popper walking with a(n) _____ [3] penguin in downtown Stillwater. They might have been less surprised if they had spotted this pair in the middle of a winter _____ [4] or on their way to a(n) _____.[5] A reporter, in his usual _____ [6] manner commented that a penguin in Stillwater in the summertime was as common as a flamingo in the Antarctic.

> Read to find out why Mr. Popper put the furnace in the living room.

Questions:

1. Why does the penguin bring Mr. Popper a checker? According to Mr. Popper, what would a penguin in the wild have done instead?
2. How does Mr. Popper solve the problem of telling the penguins apart?
3. Why does Mr. Popper's family have to wear heavy clothing indoors?
4. Why do the Poppers now have a furnace in their living room?
5. How does Mr. Popper choose the names for the baby penguins? If there had been five more babies, what do you think Mr. Popper might have named them?
6. How do the penguins entertain themselves?
7. Why does Mr. Popper dread the coming of spring?

Chapters 11, 12 (cont.)

Question for Discussion:

Do you think it is fair of Mr. Popper to require his family to endure the cold and snow inside their home?

Science Connection:

Review the Background Information on penguins on page two of this study guide and the additional research you did on penguins in the Pre-Reading Activities on page three of this study guide. Determine whether the factual information offered about penguins in Chapter Twelve is accurate.

Graphic Organizer:

The arrival of the penguins in the Popper household is a mixed blessing: it is both good and bad. Fill in the chart below telling the *pros* and *cons* of having the penguins.

What's Good About Penguins	What's Bad About Penguins

Writing Activity:

Write about a time when you were asked to sacrifice your own comfort for another. Tell why the sacrifice had to be made, whether you suffered, and if it was all worthwhile.

CHAPTERS 13, 14

Vocabulary: Read the definitions for each of the words in bold below. Then write the letter of the definition that tells how the word is used in the sentence on the line to the right.

bill

    a. piece of paper money

    b. statement of money owed

    c. bird's beak

1. The <u>bill</u> for the live fish was much larger than Mr. Popper had expected.   _____

plant

    a. complete equipment for a mechanical process

    b. any member of the vegetable group of living organisms

    c. set firmly on the ground

2. The engineer who had installed the basement freezing <u>plant</u> kept asking for money.   _____

fast

    a. securely

    b. rapidly

    c. abstain from food

3. Her tongue stuck <u>fast</u> to the cold popsicle, like a leaf to a newly tarred road.   _____

drill

    a. make a hole by boring

    b. tool for making holes in firm materials

    c. any strict methodical training

4. Mr. Popper would <u>drill</u> the penguins like a small army parading on the ice in the basement.   _____

> Read to find out why Mr. Popper thinks show business is the answer.

Questions:

1. How does Mr. Popper propose to solve the family's money problems?
2. How does Mr. Popper choose the theme for the penguins' act?
3. What evidence shows that the penguins are well trained by the time they go to see Mr. Greenbaum?
4. How do you know that Mr. Greenbaum is interested in the penguin act?

Chapters 13, 14 (cont.)

Questions for Discussion:

1. Can you think of any other ways for the Popper family to earn money?

2. Would you want to see a trained penguin act?

Music Connection:

Mrs. Popper chooses appropriate music for the penguins' three acts. Suppose the penguins were to do the following other acts, what music would you choose to accompany them? Fill in the chart below. Add another act that the penguins might perform and the music that would accompany it.

Act	Music
imitate a rock band	
ice skate	
take an automobile trip	
imitate a symphony orchestra	

Writing Activity:

Imagine you are Mr. Popper and you have been keeping a journal ever since the penguins arrived. Write a journal entry expressing your hopes and dreams on the day you take the penguins to see Mr. Greenbaum at the Palace Theater.

CHAPTERS 15, 16

Vocabulary: In each set of words below, underline the one word that does not belong. Then write a sentence explaining why it does not fit.

1. indulgence   porter   Pullman   berth

   _____

   _____

2. unique   singular   uncommon   ecstatic

   _____

   _____

3. semicircle   triangle   novelty   square

   _____

   _____

4. precision   decision   accuracy   exactness

   _____

   _____

5. turmoil   serenity   commotion   chaos

   _____

   _____

Background Information: Pullman Cars

Pullman is the trademark for the railroad sleeping car or parlor car designed by George Mortimer Pullman (1831–1897). Pullman decided that he wanted to produce a better sleeping car than anyone before him. It was quite expensive to produce the early Pullman cars in the 1860s, but Pullman decided that people would be willing to pay for comfort. The success of his sleeping cars showed that he was right. Each night the porters would pass from car to car, adjusting seats into sleeping berths. Each morning, the berths, or bunk beds, with curtains for privacy, were converted back into seats.

> Read to find out what happens when the penguins are live on stage.

Chapters 15, 16 (cont.)

Questions:

1. Why do the penguins have their audition on a real stage in front of a live audience instead of in Mr. Greenbaum's office?

2. How does the audience react when the penguins get out of control during the ladder act?

3. Why do you think Mr. Greenbaum wants the ushers to see the penguins march?

4. Why do the taxis have an accident?

5. Why don't the other performers enjoy the penguins as much as the audience enjoys them?

Questions for Discussion:

1. Why do you think Mr. Popper makes the remark that "travel is very broadening"?

2. Why do you think the penguins perform their act so well?

Writing Activity:

Imagine you are a critic for the entertainment section of the local newspaper. Write a review of the show in which the penguins performed before an audience.

CHAPTERS 17, 18

Vocabulary: Choose a word from the Word Box to complete each of the analogies below.

WORD BOX		
drowsy	huge	refuse
expensive	Philadelphia	vexed

1. ENTRANCE is to EXIT as CHEAP is to _____.

2. DETROIT is to MICHIGAN as _____ is to PENNSYLVANIA.

3. ACCEPT is to YES as _____ is to NO.

4. TINY is to SMALL as LARGE is to _____.

5. _____ is to SLEEPY as FAMOUS is to WELL KNOWN.

6. ANNOYED is to _____ as BRIEF is to SHORT.

Language Study: An idiom is an expression that does not mean exactly what it says. For example: "It rained cats and dogs" means it rained heavily. Circle the letter of the correct meaning for each of the underlined idiomatic expressions in the following sentences.

1. Traffic is <u>tied up</u> for miles at rush hour.

   a. knotted   b. slowed down   c. noisy

2. The singers were in the last act <u>on the bill</u>.

   a. on the schedule   b. to be charged   c. to be paid

3. The audience was <u>in an uproar</u> after the curtain went down.

   a. in a lion's cage   b. in disorder   c. carried skyward

4. The three girls could scarcely <u>believe their eyes</u>.

   a. see clearly   b. have confidence in   c. have faith their
                             what they saw   sight was restored

5. They worried about whether their supplies would <u>hold out</u> until help arrived.

   a. last   b. not move   c. not come in

6. We were <u>at sixes and sevens</u> when our schoolbus never came.

   a. tired and annoyed   b. delighted   c. confused and worried

Chapters 17, 18 (cont.)

> Read to find out what happens when Mr. Popper and the penguins show up
> at the wrong theater.

Questions:

1. Why are the penguins allowed to stay in hotels in the cities where they travel?

2. Why aren't the Poppers becoming rich on their performing tour?

3. Why don't the Poppers have to pay for the penguins' food any longer?

4. Why does Mr. Popper realize it is a mistake to take the penguins to the roof garden?

5. What crisis does Mr. Popper's absent-mindedness cause?

Questions for Discussion:

Do you think you would stand in line for half a mile to see the penguins perform? What
would you stand in a long line for?

Art Connection:

Design an advertisement for a magazine or billboard in which the penguins are
promoting a seafood product. Include a slogan as well as a picture.

Writing Activity:

Write about a time when you suffered from absent-mindedness or forgot to do something
important. Describe the consequences.

CHAPTERS 19, 20

Vocabulary: Draw a line from each word on the left to its definition on the right. Then use the numbered words to fill in the blanks in the sentences below.

1.	dismal	a.	ship
2.	corridor	b.	weary
3.	haggard	c.	gloomy
4.	vessel	d.	narrow passageway
5.	scuttle	e.	abandon

. . . .

1. They boarded the _____ minutes before it set sail.

2. He looked pale and _____ after his illness.

3. Our bad moods reflected the rainy, _____ weather.

4. If a storm appears, we will have to _____ our plans to go sailing.

5. Please line up in the _____ before entering the classroom.

> Read to find out whether Mr. Popper will go to the North Pole.

Questions:

1. How are Mr. Popper and his penguins rescued from jail?
2. How does Mr. Popper decide between the offers made by Mr. Klein and Admiral Drake?
3. Why does Admiral Drake want Mr. Popper to go along on the expedition?
4. How does Mrs. Popper react to her husband's decision to go to the North Pole?
5. What are some of the problems and benefits you can foresee if penguins are introduced to the Arctic?

Questions for Discussion:

1. Do you think Mr. Popper makes the right decision?
2. Do you think Mrs. Popper's reaction to her husband's decision is typical or unexpected?
3. What do you think the authors of this book are suggesting about following your dreams?

Chapters 19, 20 (cont.)

Literary Device: *Deus ex Machina*

In classic Greek drama, the *deus ex machina* is a god who uses his supernatural powers to solve all of the complicated problems just before the end of the play. This term is used today to describe anyone who enters the plot at the last crucial moment to solve all of the seemingly unsolvable problems. Who acts in this capacity in this novel? What problems are solved at the last moment?

_____

_____

_____

Writing Activity:

Write about a dream that you have for your future, even if it may seem outlandish. Describe what you might do to make your dream come true.

CLOZE ACTIVITY

The following passage has been taken from Chapter Nineteen in the book. Read it through completely, and then fill in each blank with a word that makes sense. Afterwards, you may compare your language with that of the authors.

It was very dull for the birds in jail. Wednesday came and there was still no _____ [1] from Mr. Greenbaum. Thursday, and the birds _____ [2] to droop. It was soon apparent that the _____ [3] of exercise, combined with the heat, might _____ [4] too much for them. There were no _____ [5] tricks or merry games. Even the younger _____ [6] sat all day in dismal silence, and Mr. Popper _____ [7] not cheer them up.

Mr. Popper _____ [8] a feeling that Mr. Greenbaum would _____ [9] turn up by the end of the _____, [10] to see about renewing the contract. But _____ [11] passed, without any news of him.

Saturday _____ [12] Mr. Popper got up very early and _____ [13] his hair. Then he dusted off the _____ [14] as well as he could, for he _____ [15] everything to look as presentable as possible, _____ [16] case Mr. Greenbaum should appear.

About ten o'clock _____ [17] was a sound of footsteps in the _____, [18] and a jingling of keys, and the _____ [19] of the cell was opened.

"You're free, Mr. Popper. _____ [20] a friend of yours here."

Mr. Popper stepped _____ [21] into the light with the penguins.

"You're _____ [22] in time, Mr. Greenbaum," he was about to _____ [23].

Then, as his eyes became accustomed to _____ [24] light, he looked again.

It was not Mr. Greenbaum _____ [25] stood there.

It was a great, bearded _____ [26] in a splendid uniform. Smiling, he held _____ [2] his hand to Mr. Popper.

"Mr. Popper," he said. "I am Admiral Drake."

POST-READING ACTIVITIES

1. Return to the chart you began on page seven of this study guide and add to the lists of events that are real and those that are fantasy. Compare your lists with those of your classmates.

2. Many authors begin writing with a "what if" premise. This book rests on two such premises: what if penguins were household pets, and what if penguins were introduced into the Arctic. Write your own animal short story based on one of these "what if" premises.

3. **Art Connection:** Mr. Popper enjoyed going to any movies that had to do with the Antarctic. Imagine making a movie about Mr. Popper and his penguins at the Arctic. Create the "film" by dividing a long piece of paper into "frames" and drawing a scene on each. The "movie" can be viewed through a peephole at one end of large box as the paper is pulled through two slits at the top and bottom of the other end. The back side of the box is cut off and the "film" is held up to a light.

4. Suppose Mrs. Popper were to write to an advice columnist in the local newspaper about a problem she has because of the penguins living in her house. What would Mrs. Popper's letter say? What might be the columnist's answer?

5. Write a story in which you finally get an unusual pet you have always wanted. What kind of pet would it be? Describe how you have to change your house to provide for the animal's health and comfort. Predict some of the problems and humorous situations that might arise.

6. Suppose the authors had decided to include one more zany anecdote about the penguins. Write about another funny incident that you create from your own imagination.

7. Pretend that you have been contracted to do a movie version of one episode from the story. Which episode do you think would make the best short movie? Why? Write a short screenplay for this episode. Suggest the names of performers who could play the parts and the appropriate background music.

8. **Art Connection:** Design a poster announcing that Mr. Popper and his penguins are going to perform in your town. Include information about the place, time, and date of the performance.

9. **Book Bag:** Create a "book bag" to get someone else excited about reading *Mr. Popper's Penguins*. Decorate the outside of a brown paper bag with the book title, the author's name, and a picture. Inside the bag place items or pictures of things that have something to do with the story. Give the book bag to someone before they read the book. Let this person predict what the story will be about by looking at the items in the bag.

Post-Reading Activities (cont.)

10. **Literature Circle:** Have a literature circle discussion in which you tell your personal reactions to *Mr. Popper's Penguins*. Here are some questions and sentence starters to help your literature circle begin a discussion.

    - Do you think that most of this story was realistic or that it was mainly fantasy? Which part did you like better?

    - What did you learn about penguins that you never knew before?

    - Who else would you like to read this book? Why?

    - What questions would you like to ask the author about this book?

    - It was not fair when . . .

    - I would have liked to see . . .

    - I laughed when . . .

    - I was sad when . . .

    - On a scale of 1–10, with 10 being the best, how would you rate this book? Why?

SUGGESTIONS FOR FURTHER READING

Averill, Esther. *Captains of the City Streets, a Story of the Cat Club*. HarperCollins.

* Butterworth, Oliver. *The Enormous Egg*. Scholastic.

Cleary, Beverly. *Runaway Ralph*. HarperCollins.

Clymer, Eleanor. *A Search for Two Bad Mice*. Aladdin.

* Dahl, Roald. *Danny the Champion of the World*. Puffin.

* DuBois, William Pene. *The Twenty-One Balloons*. Puffin.

* George, Jean. *My Side of the Mountain*. Puffin.

Freeman, Don. *Penguins of All People*. Viking.

Hildick, E.W. *Manhattan is Missing*. Avon.

* Juster, Norman. *The Phantom Tollbooth*. Knopf.

* King-Smith, Dick. *Babe the Gallant Pig*. Knopf.

* Lewis, C.S. *The Lion, the Witch and the Wardrobe*. Harper Collins.

* Lindren, Astrid. *Pippi Longstocking*. Penguin.

Lofting, Hugh. *The Voyages of Dr. Doolittle*. Yearling.

* Norton, Mary. *The Borrowers*. Sandpiper.

* O'Brien, Robert. *Mrs. Frisby and the Rats of NIMH*. Aladdin.

* Rockwell, Thomas. *How to Eat Fried Worms*. Yearling.

* Selden, George. *The Cricket in Times Square*. Dell.

_____. *Tucker's Countryside*. Square Fish.

* Steig, William. *Abel's Island*. Square Fish.

* White, E.B. *Charlotte's Web*. HarperCollins.

* _____. *Stuart Little*. HarperCollins.

* _____. *Trumpet of the Swan*. HarperCollins.

Wiska, Barbara. *Tunes for a Small Harmonica*. Dell.

* NOVEL-TIES Study Guides are available for these titles.

ANSWER KEY

Chapters 1, 2

Vocabulary: 1. f 2. a 3. d 4. c 5. g 6. e 7. b; 1. expedition 2. spectacles 3. expanse 4. authority 5. bungalow 6. prospect 7. missionary

Questions: 1. Mr. Popper is a frustrated scientist and explorer who would like to exchange his life as a housepainter and family man for that of an adventurer. 2. To satisfy his interest in distant places, Mr. Popper reads travel books and goes to movies about foreign lands, particularly those about the North and South Poles. 3. Since painters do not have much work during the winter, Mrs. Popper worries that funds will run low. 4. Mr. Popper learns that penguins live only at the South Pole. He theorizes that penguins would like to live at the North Pole, too. 5. Mrs. Popper is astonished because Admiral Drake addresses her husband directly in his radio message in response to a letter Mr. Popper had sent him.

Characterization: 1. inquisitive 2. absent-minded 3. impractical 4. amiable

Chapters 3, 4

Vocabulary: 1. f 2. c 3. a 4. e 5. d 6. b; Answers will vary to the second part of the vocabulary question.

Questions: 1. A penguin arrives at Mr. Popper's home as a gift mailed to him by Admiral Drake. 2. Mr. Popper names the penguin Captain Cook after the explorer who made discoveries about penguins in Antarctica. 3. The children are delighted and want to know all about the penguin, whereas Mrs. Popper seems nervous about the damage he is causing. Mrs. Popper becomes captivated by the penguin after she observes its adorable antics. 4. The penguin eats the goldfish and pecks at Mrs. Popper. The penguin is not accustomed to domestic life and is simply following its instincts. 5. To make the penguin comfortable, Mr. Popper plans to have the icebox modified as a cold environment for the penguin and to buy canned shrimp as food.

Chapters 5, 6

Vocabulary: 1. c 2. d 3. a 4. e 5. b 6. f; 1. indignant 2. remodeled 3. ordinance 4. municipal 5. marketing 6. ventilating

Questions: 1. Since Mr. Popper looks very untidy and has not told him about the penguin, the service man concludes that only an insane individual would request air holes in the refrigerator door and the installation of an inside handle. 2. The service man leaves hastily, slamming the door behind him, when the penguin starts pecking at him. 3. A policeman comes because the service man complained. The policeman suggests to Mr. Popper that he find out whether a license is required for the penguin. 4. Mr. Popper gives up trying to get a license for the penguin because no one at City Hall understands his request, and he realizes that there could not be an ordinance requiring penguins to be licensed.

Chapters 7, 8

Vocabulary: 1. e 2. a 3. b 4. g 5. c 6. d 7. f; 1. reproach 2. bystander 3. reluctantly 4. idle 5. extinct 6. abandoned 7. belated

Questions: 1. Mr. Popper explains that penguins ordinarily collect stones for their rookery, but this domesticated penguin is substituting household items. 2. Mr. Popper thinks the penguin's activity will save Mrs. Popper the never-ending household task of picking up after her family. 3. Mr. Popper's improved grooming is a reflection of the pride and excitement he feels about having a special bird. 4. As he walks with Mr. Popper, the penguin is mistaken for a goose, a pelican, and an anteater. 5. Mr. Popper finds it difficult to take the penguin for a walk because people stop out of curiosity, the bird pecks at a store window, and a newspaper photographer tries to take their picture, tangling them up in his equipment.

Chapters 9, 10

Vocabulary: 1. c 2. a 3. b 4. d 5. c

Questions: 1. The penguin is an unwelcome visitor to the barber shop because he scares away the customers and eats the teeth out of the combs. 2. Mr. Popper needs to take a nap after his walk with the penguin because he is exhausted from running up steps and being pulled down on his belly. 3. The "Shadows" are problems that begin to crop up: the penguin is becoming ill. 4. A veterinarian whom Mr. Popper consults refers him to the curator of an aquarium for advice. The curator suggests that Greta, a lonely female penguin, be brought to the Poppers' household to alleviate the mutual loneliness of the penguins.

Chapters 11, 12

Vocabulary: 1. d 2. f 3. e 4. b 5. a 6. c;.1. occupied 2. astonished 3. sleek 4. blizzard 5. rookery 6. droll

Questions: 1. Mr. Popper thinks the gift of a checker is the penguin's way of thanking him for the companionship of a female penguin. In the wild, the penguin would have offered him a stone. 2. To tell the penguins apart, Mr. Popper paints their names on their backs. 3. Since the two penguins take up the entire refrigerator, leaving no room for food, Mr. Popper moves the birds into a house that is now so cold it requires warm clothing and moves the food back to the refrigerator. 4. The Poppers have a furnace in the living room because they have turned the basement into a cold environment for the penguins and have moved the furnace upstairs to make more room. 5. The baby penguins are named after the explorers he idolizes and the monarchs they served. Answers to the second part of the question will vary. 6. To entertain themselves, the penguins toboggan, march, and spar. 7. Mr. Popper dreads spring because he will not have as much time to observe the penguins once house-painting season begins.

Chapters 13, 14
Vocabulary: 1. b   2. a   3. a   4. c
Questions: 1. To solve the family's money problems, Mr. Popper proposes that they train the penguins to perform in public for profit. 2. Mr. Popper, having observed the penguins march in the basement, decides to have them appear as an army drill team; having seen two penguins fighting, he decides to have them appear as sparring boxers; and having seen them climb and toboggan in the basement, he decides to show them as swimmers at a brook. 3. It is clear that the penguins are well trained when they march in line without leashes to visit Mr. Greenbaum. 4. It is evident that Mr. Greenbaum is interested in the penguin act when he is willing to interrupt his busy schedule to audition the penguins and when he offers Mrs. Popper the piano so that she can provide an accompaniment to the act.

Chapters 15, 16
Vocabulary: 1. indulgence–the other words relate to the railroad   2. ecstatic–the other words all mean different or unusual   3. novelty–the other words all relate to shapes   4. decision–the other words all mean correctness   5. serenity–this word is the opposite of the other three which all suggest confusion and disorganization
Questions: 1. The penguins audition on a real stage before a live audience when the members of the closing act do not show up. The penguins, therefore, have to fill in for them. 2. The audience is amused and enjoys the show even when the penguins get out of control during the ladder act. 3. Mr. Greenbaum wants his ushers to see the penguins march because he would like them to march as well as the penguins. 4. The taxis have an accident because they are racing to be the first at the station and the first to surprise people with their passengers. 5. The other performers are jealous of the penguins because they have more appeal than any of the other acts and are stealing the show.

Chapters 17, 18
Vocabulary: 1. expensive 2. Philadelphia 3. refuse 4. huge 5. drowsy 6. vexed
Language Study: 1. b   2. a   3. b   4. b   5. a   6. c
Questions: 1. The penguins are allowed to stay in hotels where they travel because there are no rules at all concerning penguins; thus, there is no justification for excluding them. 2. The Poppers are not becoming rich because the hotel bills, ice, taxis, and food are using up most of their earnings. 3. Once Mr. Popper endorses Owen's Oceanic Shrimp, he receives free shrimp for the penguins. 4. Mr. Popper is afraid that one penguin could be pushed off the roof because in the wild penguins will push one into the water to test its safety. 5. In his typical, absent-minded way, Mr. Popper brings the penguins to the wrong theater. They encounter Simpson's Seals, a rough lot. Because of the chaos that ensues, the theater manager has Mr. Popper arrested.

Chapters 19, 20
Vocabulary: 1. c   2. d   3. b   4. a   5. e; 1. vessel 2. haggard 3. dismal 4. scuttle 5. corridor
Questions: 1. Mr. Popper and his penguins are rescued from jail by Admiral Drake who sees the newspaper article and comes to bail them out. 2. Mr. Klein wants to put the birds into the movies, whereas Admiral Drake wants to take the penguins to the North Pole to start a race of penguins there. Mr. Popper chooses the latter because he thinks it represents better treatment for the birds and would enhance the existing body of scientific knowledge about the penguin. 3. Admiral Drake wants Mr. Popper to go along on the expedition because it was Mr. Popper who gave Admiral Drake the idea in his original letter. Also, Mr. Popper has proven himself to be a responsible keeper of penguins. 4. Mrs. Popper accepts her husband's decision cheerfully, saying she will miss him, but his absence will make it easier for her to clean the house. 5. Answers will vary, but one advantage could be the benefit of having more penguins to study in a new environment, while a disadvantage might be the problem of overpopulation.